# Penguin Place Value

*A Math Adventure*

*Kathleen L. Stone*

*Dedication*

*To my husband, sons, daughter-in-laws and grandchildren who give me their love, support, and inspiration. I am blessed to have all of you in my life.*

Way down south
In the snow and ice
Lived a family of penguins
Who were really quite nice

They worked hard all day
Catching fish by the shore
Placing them on trays
To take back to their store

The trays were quite handy
They really were fine
Problem is they were small
They only held *nine*

When more fish were caught
They were moved once again
To a bright yellow box
Big enough to hold *ten*

*Ten* fish to a box
Now that was the rule
And they kept them on ice
To stay nice and cool

By the end of the day
All the fish had been caught
Now it's time to find out
How many fish that they've got

Six boxes of fish
And four on a tray
Were stacked by their van
To be sent on their way

6 tens = 60

4 ones = 4

60 + 4 = 64

Six boxes make *sixty*
Now don't forget the four
That's *64* fish
To be sold at their store

Tomorrow's a new day
These fish will be bought
We hope you come back
And count new fish we've caught

# Place Value

Children need to understand and apply concepts of whole numbers. **Penguin Place Value** provides practice with the concept of **place value**. Place value helps us understand the value of a numeral (i.e. **9** has a different value in each of these numbers: 9. 90, 900, 9,000, etc.). Place value tells us if the **9** stands for nine, ninety, nine hundred, or nine thousand. Place value will also play an important role as children eventually learn how to do addition and subtraction with double- and triple-digit numbers (with and without *regrouping*).

Children should be given many opportunities to work with concrete examples (hands on manipulatives) before moving on to more abstract concepts.

## Enrichment Activities

*Materials needed:*

fish crackers (approximately 40)
paper cups
place value mat  (you can easily make your own)

*place value mat*

- ♥  Provide child with a *place value* mat … the white side will represent the *trays* (ones place), the cups are the *boxes* and the yellow side the tens place.

- ♥  Share different stories involving the penguins and fish – every fish caught must go on the tray. As soon as ten fish are caught they must be moved to a box (paper cup) and placed in the yellow tens place.

- ♥  Your child can use the fish to represent specific numbers that you give them (i.e. "Show me 27 fish.").

- ♥  You may also put the fish on the place value mat and have your child tell you how many there are. For example, you place three cups of fish on the tens side (10 fish in each cup) and 6 on the ones side. Ask your child, "How many fish did the penguin catch today?" and your child would answer "36."

- ♥  Add further enrichment by having your child write the numeral shown.

# ABOUT THE AUTHOR

Kathleen Stone is a National Board Certified educator and is currently teaching second grade. She loves spending time with her family. She and her husband Gary live in the Olympia area. When not teaching, Kathleen can often be found quilting or sitting by the lake reading!

Math is all around us
No matter where you turn
Open your mind to the wonders of math
And all that you can learn

Made in the USA
Monee, IL
28 February 2020